ISSI  I0051880

Dediu Newsletter

Author: Michael M. Dediu

World Monthly Report
News and Suggestions for Sustainable
Peace, Freedom and Prosperity

Vol. 4, Nr. 12 (48), 6 November 2020

DERC Publishing House
Nashua, New Hampshire, U. S. A.
For subscriptions please use the contact form at www.derc.com

Published and printed in the
United States of America
On the Great Seal of the United States are included:
E Pluribus Unum (Out of many, one)
Annuit Coeptis (He has approved of the undertakings)
Novus Ordo Seclorum (New order of the ages)

Dediu, Michael M.

Dediu Newsletter Vol 4, Number 12 (48), 6 November 2020
World Monthly Report with news and suggestions for Sustainable Peace, Freedom and Prosperity

ISSN 2475-2061
ISBN 978-1-950999-24-8

Preface

Generally, people are optimistic, because they instinctively know that leaders who work for peace, freedom, good health, harmony and prosperity, and who are honest, modest and inspire trust – will ultimately succeed.

From a world sustainable peace, good health, freedom and prosperity point of view, this October 2020 had - beside the disturbing news of great increases in war-related expenses and preparations – the unusually complicated COVID-19 pandemic continues to be a serious medical issue, which shows the need for a unified world, focused on the health, wellbeing and freedom of all people. Now some good news: a team at Vanderbilt University developed a back-assist exosuit; specialists make bioplastics based on a polymer called polylactic acid (PLA), which allows plastics to be biodegradable; Amazon will hire 100,000 seasonal workers for holidays; using artificial intelligence and MRI scans researchers identified signs of osteoarthritis three years before diagnosis; portable sequencing is making it possible for geneticists to bring the lab to the field.

In this World Monthly Report, which is the 48th in total, we included the most relevant news, in a balanced approach, usually directly from the source, to help the general public better understand the realities around us. Being well and correctly informed is a sine qua non requirement for everybody, in order to make the right decisions for the future, which future begins to take shape in our recent books. This World Monthly Report provides the information needed for making the best-informed decisions.
Enjoy this World Monthly Report, and be optimist!

Michael M. Dediu, Ph. D.

Nashua, NH, U. S. A., 6 November 2020

USA, New York: On 7th Avenue at West 57th Street, looking southwest: right: a classical building, which is tangent to the right, on W 57th St, to the American Fine Arts Society building (1892); left down: a beautiful building, opposite Carnegie Hall (to the left, across 7th Ave, 1891, concert hall with exceptional acoustics, architecture and performance history); left up: an impressive double skyscraper, with the southwest side on W 56th St.

Table of Contents

Italy, 29 September 2008, Venezia (421), Piazza San Marco (1084) Libreria Sansoviniana. (1468-1560, left), Campanile (850, 1514, 1912, 99 m, back), Torre dell'Orologio (1499, back), San Theodore Column (1268), Basilica di San Marco (1156-1173, right).

World Status Report
3 November 2020

Reports: COVID-19 brings more job losses and business closures than 2008 crisis.

October is Health Literacy Month for all people.

Rising coronavirus cases around the world are hurting all people – they all ask for better world health research and care, as mentioned in the new World Constitution.

The personality cult is still alive in many countries, but it is temporary, until the people will change everything.

People want a global rethinking of priorities, focusing on peace, freedom, health, education, harmony and prosperity.

People do not like the deep division in the world, the fact that the conversations between leaders are degrading into fracturing, and civility is sapping — all these increase the probability of large confrontations.

People are working to get our world on the right track – peace, freedom, health, harmony and prosperity, the only way to have a robust and sustainable future.

People want to have at the heart of the world economy people, peace, freedom, health, education, harmony and prosperity.

All people would like to see all countries committed towards net zero war-related products and expenses by 2022, and transforming all war-related industries to peace-related production, creating thus over 10,000,000 jobs in the world.

The hospital of the future in the world will frequently use AI for many medical tasks.

Pediatric and geriatric medicine are important in the world.

Transitioning from war-programs to peace-programs is a priority for all.

There are heightened stresses today, because of the war risks.

Portable technology offers rapid, point-of-care cancer diagnosis, and is essential for many in the world.

Tenacity and willpower are needed for peace, freedom, health and prosperity for all.

Mentorship for younger generation is useful, in order to learn about self-care and lifelong learning

Peace, freedom, health, education and technology are propelling humanity to a better future.

There is international research on the social determinants of health, created by the difficulties of having peace and freedom.

Global online auctions bring all people together.

Global opportunities help to build and live a happier and more fulfilling life.

Quick access to products and services will help everybody expedite design, prototyping, development processes, and have a better life

The solar power will become more important in the world's electricity production.

Early childhood education is very important in the world.

During this year's National Protect Your Hearing Month—observed each October—it is important to learn how to protect yourself and your loved ones from noise-induced hearing loss (NIHL), and help Noisy Planet spread the word to others

All people want the Noisy Planet to be transformed in the Quiet Planet.

Quality Consumer Products are difficult to find, and this is a serious issue.

October 13th is International Plain Language Day, an NIH's plain language page has information about tools, training and other resources.

The world economic outlook is not good now – much more effort should be allocated to improve it.
Global Financial Stability Report: not good, too much deficit, not enough jobs, too much war-related expenses.
Fiscal Monitor: printing too much money.
Global economy should be focused on helping people, not in more arms to kill them.

People want to de-risk their savings, and get 5% interest at their banks.

People applaud the global organizations which work to improve the quality of life for many people on the planet.

People want from CEOs to be friendly, work for peace, freedom, good health, good education, harmony, and prosperity for all.

Globally, polio cases have been reduced by 99.9% thanks to the many health workers, community leaders, and volunteers, who have never lost sight of reaching every last child.

All people should be automatically registered to vote, based on the information available, not create another bureaucratic process, just to waste more of people's time and money.

The world election day will be a day of celebration and harmony for all.

People are looking very confident ten years ahead: in the one country Peaceful Terra, they will have key converging technologies in computing, data, and analysis - this will help the world governance, standards, and norms in knowledge and privacy. Without any borders, data will flow freely, for the benefit of everybody.

Daily there are new needs emerging around the world.

The global medical device contract manufacturing and engineering market is estimated at $52.9 B in 2019, and expected to nearly double through 2025.

29 October 2020 is World Stroke Day - about 25% of the people have a stroke.

People are interested in root cause analysis for many world problems – including failure investigation, product complaint, non-conformance, hazard analysis, risk management, and mitigation activities.

People in many countries are again abused with the superfluous change of hour, which creates many difficulties, waste of time and energy, etc. – the people want to stop these abuses, and concentrate to work together for peace, freedom, good health, good education, no abuses, harmony and prosperity.

On 31st of October, many people celebrate the 173rd anniversary of the birthday of the Italian physicist Galileo Ferraris (31 Oct 1847 – 7 Feb 1897, only 49.2 years old), who established the basic principle of AC power system and of the induction motor, which is now the principal device for the conversion of electrical power to mechanical power, used now by everybody in the world.

The Sun – and our whole solar system - orbits around the center of the Milky Way Galaxy. We are moving at an average velocity of 230 km/sec, and it takes us about 230 millions of years to make one complete orbit around the Milky Way. This rotation around the center of the Milky Way Galaxy, at 230 km/s, creates the sinusoidal climate changes often observed on Earth.

The World Constitution Day is 6 March.

Important for all countries: over 59 years ago, in Dwight D. Eisenhower's farewell speech, on January 17, 1961, the former famous Five Star General in the Army, Supreme Commander of the Allied Forces in Europe in World War II, and the 34th President of the United States warned of the dangers of allowing a Military-Industrial Complex to take control: "In the councils of government, we must guard against the acquisition of unwarranted influence, whether sought or unsought, by the military–industrial complex". The Military-Industrial Complex is a term that denotes an interdependent relationship between a nation's military, economy, and politics, and it is valid for all nations.

Everywhere in the world mediation should be a much better alternative to the courts.

All people are gentle by birth – that gentleness must be cultivated and increased over the years.

Alignment towards a common goal is key to success in a good world government. All government employees should feel connected, empowered and ready to run for each other and the people and government goal.

Global resilience is remarkable, because people want better future for all.

Good leaders do not micromanage everything – they remember Ronald Reagan: "In this present crisis, government is not the solution to our problems; government is the problem."

The world government will be in near-constant conversation with people, always asking how to help.

Good music and art are important for the world.

In many countries, the money printers are running non-stop, which is very bad, and will generate high inflation.

Jefferson reminds all people: "All tyranny needs to gain a foothold is for people of good conscience to remain silent."

People remember Thucydides: Ignorance is bold and knowledge reserved.
And Leonardo da Vinci: Nothing strengthens authority so much as silence.

Noise is bad for people's health, and for people's ability to think – noise hurts people's cognitive performance. Noise will be stopped with advanced technology.

Over 360,000 babies are born each day in the world, over 130 M per year.

Friendly pro-democracy and pro-global peace activities are increasing in the world.

There are around 2 billions of families in the world, and they all want peace, freedom and prosperity for them, for their children and grandchildren.

People ask to have AI, satellites and space used only for peaceful purposes.

There is a complete disconnect between the economy (down) and the heavily manipulated stock market (up).

Global security is real only if there are no arms at all.

World quality of life index: 2.1 (bad) (1 very bad, 10 excellent)

World medical assistance index: 2 (bad) (1 very bad, 10 excellent)

The State of Communications in World Healthcare - Broken
World noise level: unhealthy

World Financial Stability Index: 2 (1 very bad, 10 excellent)

World Food Stability Index: 3 (1 very bad, 10 excellent)

World Freedom Stability Index: 2 (1 very bad, 10 excellent)

Electrical Safety Standards Worldwide – good
Business Expectations Index – low
Business Uncertainty Index – high
- Global security threats increased.
- Global relationships are unstable.
- Global monetary policy is not good.
- Global economic outlook is unstable.
- Global inflationary overheating is taking place.
- Saving Humanity from war is a major objective for the 7.7 B people on Earth.

The world borderlands are always in danger, with many conflicts every single day.

Misinformation, disinformation and mal-information are everywhere in the world these days.

Fiscal irresponsibility is very common these days.

United States of America

(Population 330 M, rank 3, growth 0.5%. Free: 89 of 100. Area 9.52 M km^2, rank 4.).

Short Status Report:

The third president of the United States, Thomas Jefferson, said about 195 years ago, in 1825: "I know no safe depository of the ultimate powers of the society but the people themselves. This is the true corrective of abuses of constitutional power."

Reports: U.S. Stocks are artificially overvalued.
Over the last 40 years, U.S. equities have had roughly the same P/E ratio as the rest of the world. Over the last 10, the U.S. have produced massively inflated performance relative to its global peers, with valuations becoming increasingly stretched. One actually has to go back to the 1920s to find a period where U.S. stock valuations were this stretched relative to their global peers.

Reports: September 2020 job cut total is 186% higher than September 2019. Job cuts announced by U.S.-based employers jumped to 118,804 in September, up 2.6% from August's total of 115,762, according to a monthly report released Thursday, 1 Oct. Last month's job cuts bring the yearly total so far to 2,082,262, up 348% from the 464,869 cuts at this time last year. 5 M older workers lost jobs in the period March-June.

2 October 2020. Reports: President Trump tweeted he and Melania Trump have begun to quarantine, after testing positive for the coronavirus.

Reports: The U.S. Treasury is the biggest borrower in the world.

6 October 2020. Reports: The U.S.'s international trade deficit in goods and services increased to $67.1 billions in August from $63.4 billions in July (revised), as imports increased more than exports.

With an annual budget of $477 M, the National Institute of Dental and Craniofacial Research has an impact on oral health. All people applaud the new Director of NIDCR: "NIDCR's community will continue to deliver on our mission, one I am proud to say I have always shared: to improve dental, oral, and craniofacial health…for all."

Reports: August 2020 deficit: $200 B.

Current 11 months deficit: $3.007 T – the previous 12 months deficit was $0.984 T.

Federal Reserve is contributing to deficits and artificial stock inflation, benefiting those with many stocks.

Reports: The increase for COLA (cost-of-living adjustment), for federal retirement annuities and Social Security benefits, will be 1.3% for 2021. It's the lowest COLA in four years, and it falls far short of what the millions of federal retirees need. The cost of health care continues to rise over 6% per year, faster than other goods and services (around 5% per year), and seniors spend more on medical care than those under the age of 62.

Low interest rates are also a big difficulty for retirees today.

Political ad spending is over $6.7 B per election, therefore people's money is transferred to local TV – not good for people.

Reports: On October 14, the Office of Personnel Management (OPM) announced that Federal Employees Health Benefits (FEHB) program premiums, for enrolled active and retired federal employees, will increase by an average of 4.9% in 2021. This increase could become a source of financial stress for some federal employees and their families, because of the 1% federal pay increase for 2021. Likewise, federal retirees will bear the pain of higher premiums as their purchasing power continues to ebb from stagnant cost-of-living adjustments (COLAs). For these annuitants, the 1.3%

COLA in 2021 falls short of what's needed to cover the increase in FEHB premiums and other health care expenses.

Reports: The U.S. could authorize emergency use of Moderna's experimental COVID-19 vaccine in December, according to CEO Stéphane Bancel, if the company gets positive interim results in November from a large clinical trial. The comments suggest Moderna's timetable isn't that far off from Pfizer's, which said last week it expects to seek U.S. authorization of emergency use of its vaccine by late November. The latest news comes as two other leading COVID-19 vaccines, from Johnson & Johnson and AstraZeneca, have been paused, as the companies investigate illnesses among study subjects.

Reports: The Congressional Budget Office's budget projections over the next 30 years: between FY 2021 and FY 2050, federal spending will grow as more Americans retire, structural budget deficits will worsen, and the share of the debt held by the public will rise to unprecedented levels. But the projections weren't limited to the budget. The Congressional Budget Office (CBO) also looked at economic and labor trends. Those are just as alarming as the budget projections.

Earlier this year, the Census Bureau released population data showing that the natural increase in population (births minus deaths) dropped below 1 million "for the first time in decades." Including immigration, the population grew by 1.552 million. Live births declined in 42 states and the District of Columbia. Only eight states experienced an increase in live births. Deaths outnumbered live births in four states -- West Virginia, Maine, New Hampshire, and Vermont.

8 millions of Americans slipped into poverty amid coronavirus pandemic, new study says.

About 40% of children live in a household struggling to afford basics.

The U.S. reported a record of more than 83,000 new COVID infections on both Friday, 23 Oct and Saturday, 24 Oct.

PG&E is pre-emptively cutting power again in northern California, affecting 386,000 homes and businesses in 38 counties, or nearly 1 M people. It's the fourth times this year the state's largest utility had to shut off electricity due to high winds and extreme wildfire danger, which could spark blazes if live wires topple into dry brush. Utilities in Southern California, like Southern California Edison, are also warning of potential blackouts.

History report: 35 years ago, when President Ronald Reagan met with Soviet leader Mikhail Gorbachev in 1985, Republican Rep. Newt Gingrich called it "the most dangerous summit for the West since Adolf Hitler met with Neville Chamberlain in 1938 in Munich." Yet, Reagan's and Gorbachev's roles in ending the Cold War through diplomacy would become their most significant legacy.

Report: "Every year, throughout the United States, thousands of citizens are being abused by a growingly authoritarian federal government. The sheer volume of federal statutes and regulations that carry criminal penalties means that every American could be considered a criminal by federal authorities for one thing or another."

Reports: The US 2020 deficit is at $3.1 T and climbing.
Deficit spending has become the crack cocaine for professional investors.

The US public sector added 344,000 jobs last month – including 95,000 permanent state and local jobs, 11,000 permanent federal jobs, and 238,000 Census jobs -

From David Stockman (Republican U.S. Representative from Michigan (1977–1981), and the Director of the Office of Management and Budget (1981–1985) under President Ronald Reagan): the US economy is imperiled by $74 trillions of public and private debt, and egregious Wall Street bubbles whose days are clearly numbered.

The fourth president of the United States from 1809 to 1817, James Madison, said about 190 years ago, in 1830: "The means of defense agst. foreign danger, have been always the instruments of tyranny at home."
"The advancement and diffusion of knowledge is the only guardian of true liberty."

Over 10,000 babies are born each day in the U.S., over 3.6 M per year.

"A federal program dumps money from the top, and these blue-chip companies steal it all," said a Mayor of a small town.

Ballooning budget deficit and ballooning stock market go hand in hand.

- Financial responsibility is very low.
- Current overall inflation: 5.75%. It is high, under pressure, and expected to grow to 6.55 %.
- Credit risk is high.
- Market risk is very high.
- Asset prices are artificially inflated.
- Violent crimes are rising annually
- People should receive 5% interest for their deposits in banks.
- Economic outlook: unfavorable
- There is no Internet in 15% of the U.S. homes – 1 in 7 homes is without Internet.
- The U.S. student debt is over $1.6 T.
There are 44.5 millions of seniors on Social Security.
Because of the production and sales of arms, mass shootings continue, and thousands of people are killed and wounded each year.

Puerto Rico: (Population 3.6 M, rank 134, decrease 0.1%; an unincorporated territory of the United States, located in the northeast Caribbean Sea, 1,600 km southeast of Miami, Florida.).

United Nations. (UN) There are 195 officially recognized countries. Around 44,000 people work for the United Nations. There is a wide range of jobs: Researchers, IT-specialists, lawyers, experts on finance and administration, or translators work at the New York headquarters, at the official locations, or at specialized agencies. More than half of the UN's workforce is employed in the field, in projects of humanitarian aid, or on peace missions.

History: In 1945, Harold Stassen publicly proposed a nuclear-armed UN air force as a way to control the bomb, stop proliferation, and strengthen the United Nations. Although the Truman Administration rejected Stassen's proposal at the time, the idea of a nuclear-armed UN persisted into the Eisenhower and Kennedy administrations, interacting with other proposals and debates about the UN's role in nuclear decision-making and general and complete disarmament.

World Trade Organization

G20 group members are European Union (EU) and 19 countries: Argentina, Australia, Brazil, Canada, China, France, Germany, India, Indonesia, Italy, Japan, Mexico, Republic of Korea, Republic of South Africa, Russia, Saudi Arabia, Turkey, United Kingdom, United States of America.

The Group of Seven (G7) is a group consisting of Canada, France, Germany, Italy, Japan, the United Kingdom, and the United States. The G8 format (the G7 and Russia) had been in place for 16 years, from 1998-2014.

China, Japan, and neighbors

China: (Population 1.4 B, rank 1, growth 0.4%. Freedom House reports for 2020: Not Free (10 of 100). Area 9.59 M km^2, rank 3).

Reports: Chinese authorities are set to expand a high-risk program to administer experimental COVID-19 vaccines to large swaths of the population before late-stage studies are completed, aimed at rapidly advancing the products into the marketplace, and dominating global supply. Last month, a representative of state-owned China National Biotec Group, or Sinopharm, revealed that hundreds of thousands of Chinese had already taken the company's two lead vaccine candidates under the government's limited use program.

11 October 2020. Xinhua: Chinese President Xi Jinping on Saturday, 10 Oct, called on young officials to strengthen their capabilities of solving practical problems, be willing to act, and be able to deliver real outcomes. Xi, also general secretary of the Communist Party of China (CPC) Central Committee and chairman of the Central Military Commission, made the remarks while addressing the opening of a training session for young and middle-aged officials at the Party School of the CPC Central Committee (National Academy of Governance). History was advanced by addressing problems, Xi stressed, noting that by leading the people in the revolution, construction, and reform, the Party aims all about solving practical problems in the nation.

In face of the current complex situation and arduous task, Xi said it is an urgent need for officials to strengthen their capability in solving problems, adding that it is also an inevitable requirement for the young officials to grow. Officials, especially the young ones, must strengthen their political ability, and other capabilities in terms of research and study, scientific decision-making, advancing in-depth reforms, emergency responses, engaging with the people, and implementing policies, Xi said.

Xi also called on them to face up to problems, be willing to act and ready to deliver good results, and tackle difficulties.

The Party and the state undertakings have witnessed historic achievements and changes since the 18th national congress of the CPC thanks to our focus on solving problems and other important experiences, Xi said. He reminded officials that the world today is undergoing substantial changes unseen in a century, with instability and uncertainty in the external environment on the rise.

China has entered a new development phase and needs to resolve increasingly diverse and complicated problems in its endeavors to implement the new development philosophy and build new development patterns, Xi said. Though the country has scored major strategic achievements in containing the COVID-19 epidemic, he noted, steady efforts are still needed to secure a decisive victory in building a moderately prosperous society in all respects, and eradicating poverty across China.

Xi said efforts are also needed to ensure stability on six fronts -- employment, the financial sector, foreign trade, foreign investment, domestic investment, and expectations -- while maintaining security in six areas: job security, basic living needs, operations of market entities, food and energy, stable industrial and supply chains, and the normal functioning of primary-level governments.

Xi underscored the significance for young officials to be more capable in seven fields, urging them to pay paramount attention to improving their political competence to get their jobs done.

To improve political competence, young officials must maintain the correct political direction and uphold Party leadership and the Chinese socialist system, Xi said.

"There is no room for confusion or wavering on this matter," Xi stressed, urging young officials to hold the Party's political discipline and rules in awe and respect. Xi also asked young officials to improve their ability to conduct investigations and research, and hone their competence in the process.

Investigations and research should be done regularly, Xi said, adding that young officials should heed the opinions, concerns, and aspirations of the people, and learn about actual situations.

Stressing improvement in young officials' capacity in scientific decision-making, Xi asked them to hold a strategic vision and integrate the work of localities and departments into the cause of the Party and the country. Xi also urged carrying out in-depth studies and full analyses before making a decision, as well as listening to suggestions from multiple sectors. Young officials should improve their ability to tackle challenges in in-depth reforms, Xi noted, demanding efforts to deepen comprehensive reform for advancing the work of the Party and the country, especially remaining committed to the new development philosophy, promoting high-quality development, and building new development patterns.

Reforms must be advanced with courage and determination, Xi said, asking for combining the enthusiasm in work with the spirit of science, adopting correct methods and innovative thinking, as well as respecting people's pioneering spirit.

Xi urged young officials to improve emergency response capacity and risk awareness, and stand ready to cope with all kinds of risks and challenges and become experts in their fields.

They must improve the capability of engaging with the people and always care about the people's security and well-being, Xi said, stressing the principle of "from the people, to the people."

Xi called for concrete achievements in leading the people to achieve prosperity through hard work, stressing better incomes, employment, education, social security, medical insurance, medical services, and housing for the people.

Young officials should also improve the capability to implement policies, Xi said, calling for officials to be down-to-earth, take the lead in actions, and break new ground by solving difficult problems. They should take action, shoulder responsibilities, and be committed to the great practice of socialism with Chinese characteristics in the new era, an era for making things happen, said Xi.

Xi asked Party organizations at all levels to take targeted measures to help young officials grow politically, practically and professionally, so that they will be more capable of solving practical problems and performing their duties in the new era.

Wang Huning, a member of the Standing Committee of the Political Bureau of the CPC Central Committee, and a member of the Secretariat of the CPC Central Committee, attended the event.

Reports: All the people in the world expect China – with its great and friendly people – to be an example for all in working for peace (including complete disarmament), freedom, good health, good education, harmony and prosperity for all.

25 October 2020, Xinhua: Chinese President Xi Jinping has expressed high expectations for art teachers and students to inherit and develop traditional Chinese opera.

Xi, also general secretary of the Communist Party of China Central Committee and chairman of the Central Military Commission, made the remarks in a letter dated Oct. 23 to teachers and students from the National Academy of Chinese Theatre Arts.

Learning about the achievements made by the academy, Xi said he was very gratified and extended his sincere greetings to all teachers, students and staff members.

Stressing that traditional Chinese opera is the treasure of Chinese culture, Xi said that the emphasis should be placed on its practitioners to prosper and develop Chinese opera.

Xi encouraged the teachers and students of the academy to explore the true meaning of art through teaching and studying, and to constantly consolidate their original aspirations in pursuing art through serving the people. He also called on them to make greater contributions to passing on the fine traditional Chinese culture and building China into a country with a strong socialist culture.

Founded in 1950, the academy - formerly an experimental school under the then Ministry of Culture - is the first state-organized Chinese opera educational institution established after the founding of New China.

Reports: "China has purchased approximately 71% of its farm purchases target for 2020," according to an interim report on agricultural trade from the U.S. Trade Representative. "They have purchased $23.6 B in agricultural products so far this year, substantially more than the base year of 2017, and should end up being our best year ever in sales to China. It is worth noting that the Phase One Agreement did not go into effect until February 14, 2020, and March is the first full month of its effect. We already are on pace to have all-time high sales to China in beef, pork, corn, and soybeans."

31 October 2020. Xinhua: Xi Jinping, general secretary of the Communist Party of China (CPC) Central Committee, made an important speech at a symposium the Party leadership held to solicit opinions from non-Party members on drafting proposals to formulate a blueprint for China's economic and social development.

Xi presided over the symposium, held on Aug. 25, for drafting the CPC Central Committee's proposals for formulating the 14th Five-Year Plan (2021-2025) for National Economic and Social Development and the Long-Range Objectives Through the Year 2035. Members of the central committees of non-CPC political parties in China and the All-China Federation of Industry and Commerce, as well as personages with no party affiliations, gave their views and suggestions. Xi said drafting good development proposals for the 14th Five-Year-Plan period will inform the public of the major targets, areas of priority and key tasks for China's development in the next five years, noting that such proposals will pool strength for scoring new and even greater achievements in advancing the country's economic and social development.

Xi called for summarizing and reviewing the achievements and experience of the 13th Five-Year Plan period to propose significant measures for furthering reform and opening up and draft forward-thinking response plans for major risks.

Xi praised non-CPC members for the valuable comments and suggestions they had submitted during previous solicitations, and hoped that they would continue to offer their inputs as well as contribute their wisdom to formulating the 14th Five-Year Plan.

Xi called for efforts to take the initiative and rise to challenges, turn risks into opportunities, address a host of structural, cyclical and institutional problems with impact on high-quality development, and nurture new, strong and lasting driving forces for economic growth. He also emphasized establishing a new development pattern, continuing to expand domestic demand, attracting global resources and fostering new advantages in global economic cooperation and competition.

Reports: People appreciate that President Xi "praised non-CPC members for the valuable comments and suggestions they had submitted during previous solicitations, and hoped that they would continue to offer their inputs as well as contribute their wisdom". All people hope that President Xi will intensify collaboration with non-CPC members, who are a great majority, and have very useful ideas for a better China, working with other big and small countries for peace, freedom, good health, good education, good information, harmony and prosperity for all.

Hong Kong. (Population 7.3 M, rank 104, growth 0.8%. Partly Free: 61 of 100).

Macau (Population 622 K, rank 167, growth 1.7 %.)

Taiwan: (Population 23.6 M, rank 56, growth 0.3%. Free, 91 of 100).

Reports: Not paying any attention to China's recent sanctions, the U.S. State Department has signaled its approval for a potential $2.4 B sale of anti-ship missiles to Taiwan. As many as 100 Harpoon Coastal Defense Systems built by Boeing could be shipped. On Monday, 26 Oct, Beijing said it would impose sanctions on Boeing's defense unit, Lockheed Martin, and Raytheon over another $1.8 B arms sales to Taiwan, an island with which it has not ruled out the use of force to achieve reunification.

Japan (Population 127.5 M, rank 11, decrease 0.2%. Free, 96 of 100).

Reports: Japan is running some tests at the beginning of November, with three daily baseball games played at the 32 K-seat Yokohama Stadium at 80% to 100% capacity. Engineers have installed dozens of high-resolution cameras and sensors across the stadium, to monitor mask-wearing and the movements of fans, while CO_2 detectors will be used to measure crowd density, and spectators are encouraged to use apps to track who they come into contact. The huge amount of data will be inputted into Japan's Fugaku supercomputer for analysis on how the virus may spread outdoors. Japan already has a strong record on COVID-19 prevention with only 1.7 K deaths.

Afghanistan: (Population 35.5 M, rank 40, growth 2.5%. Not free: 24 of 100).

South Korea: (Population 50.9 M, rank 27, growth 0.4%. Free, 82 of 100).

Korea is the United States top export market for pomegranates.

Samsung is world's biggest producer of smartphones, TVs and memory chips.

48 people have died in South Korea after receiving flu shots, leading several physicians to call for a pause in immunizations.

North Korea: (Population 25.4 M, rank 52, growth 0.5%. Not free: 3 of 100).

Vietnam (Population 95.5 M, rank 15, growth 1%. Not free, 20 of 100, Socialist Republic of Vietnam).

Laos (Population. 6.8 M, rank 106, growth 1.5%. Not free: 12 of 100).

Cambodia (Population 16 M, rank 71, growth 1.5%. Not Free 31 of 100).

Mongolia (Population 3 M, rank 137, growth 1.6%. Free 85 of 100)

Nepal: (Population 29.3 M, rank 48, growth 1.1%. Partly free 52 of 100).

The Ammonoosuc River running south towards back, with part of the southeast side of the Mount Washington Resort (1902, right).

Russia, Switzerland, Eastern Europe

Russia: (Population 146 M, rank 9, growth 0%. Not free: 20 of 100. Area 17 M km², rank 1)

2 October 2020. Vladimir Putin sent a message of encouragement to the President of the United States of America, Donald Trump, wishing him and the First Lady a speedy recovery and expressing sincere support at this difficult moment. "I am sure that your inherent vitality, vigor and optimism will help you overcome the dangerous virus," the President of Russia wrote.

Reports: Adolf P. Shvedchikov, Ph. D. in Chemical Physics, graduated from Moscow University in 1960, worked at the Institute of Chemical Physics in Moscow, then later worked in Encino, California, USA, as general chemist at·Pulsatron Technology Corporation; also a romantic poet, wrote several poetry books in English, Russian and other languages, passed away on 17 October 2020, in California, USA, at 83.

Switzerland: (Population 8.4 M, rank 99, growth 0.9%. Free: 96 of 100).

The Swiss genomics firm SOPHiA Genetics is working on the global rollout of the company's precision medicine technology for improving the treatment of cancer and genetic disorders. In particular, SOPHiA aims to expand into hospitals in the US and Asia.

Austria: (Population 8.7 M, rank 98, growth 0.3%. Free: 95 of 100).

Poland: (Population 38.1 M, rank 37, decrease 0.1%. Free: 89 of 100).

Croatia: (Population 4.1 M, rank 129, decrease 0.6%. Free: 87 of 100).

Reports: Croatia is a net food importer.

Finland: (Population 5.5 M, rank 116, growth 0.4%. Free: 100 of 100).

The Finnish startup Rappta Therapeutics works on the development of first-in-class cancer treatments. The company's drugs are designed to activate a protein called PP2A, which suppresses tumors which are very hard to target with drugs.

Romania (Population: 19.6 M, rank 59, decrease 0.5%. Free: 84 of 100)

Reports: The Government of Romania (GOR) recently approved direct payments for farmers to compensate for COVID-19 losses, particularly in the livestock and horticultural sectors. Funded by both national and European Union (EU) budgets, the subsidies will vary according to the farm size and type.

Reports: A Romanian robot kills the coronavirus with UV light.

Moldova: (Population: 4 M, rank 132, decrease 0.2%. Partly Free: 62 of 100).

Reports: EBRD, EIB and E5P back kindergarten refurbishment in Chisinau, Moldova.

Belarus: (Population: 9.4 M, rank 93, decrease 0.1%. Not Free: 20 of 100).

Bulgaria: (Population: 7 M, rank 105, decrease 0.7%. Free: 80 of 100).

Reports: Bulgaria imports and sales of U.S. tree nuts in marketing year (MY) 2019/20 are above MY 2018/19 year, despite the challenging market dynamics. U.S. almond exports to Bulgaria during the first nine months of MY 2019/20 were at $8.3 millions, a 43% increase over the same period in MY 2018/19.

Slovenia: (Population: 2 M, rank 148, growth 0.1%. Free: 92 of 100).

Slovakia: (Population: 5.4 M, rank 117, growth 0.1%. Free: 89 of 100).

Hungary: (Population: 9.7 M, rank 91, decrease 0.3%. Free: 76 of 100)

Ukraine: (Population: 44.2 M, rank 32, decrease 0.5%. Partly free: 61 of 100).

6 October 2020. In Novo-Ogaryovo, Russia, the Russian President met with Head of the Political Council of the Ukrainian party Opposition Platform – For Life, Viktor Medvedchuk.

President of Russia Vladimir Putin: Mr Medvedchuk, I am pleased to have you here. I have known for a long time now that, despite the many challenges, you maintain a straightforward position on restoring Ukrainian-Russian relations at all levels, including state, non-governmental, and in the economy.

We are pleased to know that there are political forces in Ukraine that openly and honestly hold this position. For our part, we are ready to contribute to restoring Russian-Ukrainian relations in every way. We hope that you will have more supporters in this regard over time. To reiterate, for our part, we will do our best to restore our relations. I would like to note that we in Russia also noticed how the 75th anniversary of Victory over Nazism was celebrated in Ukraine this year. I am aware that this is largely due to your efforts, and the efforts of your associates and your party. I am confident that many people in Ukraine are grateful to you for this.

Since this is our common victory, I would like to express our gratitude to you on behalf of the Russian people.

Viktor Medvedchuk: Thank you very much, Mr Putin.

You are right about the celebration of the 75th anniversary of our common victory, the victory of the Soviet people and the Soviet Union. This is exactly how Ukrainian veterans see it. Indeed, we did our best, despite the political crisis, despite the fact that the 'party of war' is still strong in Ukraine, and despite the fact that the radicals tried in every possible way to disrupt the May 9 celebrations.

We gave our veterans the respect they deserve. We owe a debt of gratitude to them. Ukraine is home to 13,243 veterans of the Great Patriotic War. This number includes both those who fought and those who worked on the home front. We are talking about elderly people who need assistance. We did our best to bring the holiday to their homes under the current circumstances in Ukraine, and we wanted to pay tribute to them.

Latvia: (Population: 1.9 M, rank 150, decrease 1.1%. Free: 87 of 100).

Lithuania: (Population: 2.8 M, rank 141, decrease 0.6%. Free: 91 of 100).

Estonia: (Population: 1.3 M, rank 155, decrease 0.2%. Free: 94 of 100).

Serbia: (including Kosovo: Population: 8.7 M, rank 97, decrease 0.3%. Free: 76 of 100.
Kosovo ((Disputed: recognized by 110 countries, and not recognized by Serbia, Russia, and others) Population: 1.8 M, Partly free: 52 of 100).

Bosnia and Herzegovina: (Population: 3.5 M, rank 135, decrease 0.3%. Partly free: 55 of 100).

Turkey: (Population 83.7 M, rank 19, growth 1.2%, Partly free: 38 of 100).

14 October 2020. Vladimir Putin had a telephone conversation with President of the Republic of Turkey Recep Tayyip Erdogan, at the Turkish side's initiative.

The presidents discussed in detail developments in the Nagorno-Karabakh conflict zone. Both sides reaffirmed the importance of complying with the humanitarian truce that was agreed in Moscow on October 10. Vladimir Putin and Recep Tayyip Erdogan spoke in favor of stepping up the political process, in particular, based on the work of the OSCE Minsk Group.

Vladimir Putin expressed serious concern over the involvement of Middle Eastern fighters in the military action. The leaders stressed the urgent need for joint efforts in order to cease the bloodshed and move to a peaceful settlement of the Nagorno-Karabakh problem as soon as possible. Hope was expressed that Turkey, as a member of the OSCE Minsk Group, would make a constructive contribution to de-escalating the conflict. The effectiveness of cooperation between Russia and Turkey was pointed out during the discussion of Syrian and Libyan affairs. The cooperation helped to stabilize the situation and move forward on the political and diplomatic tracks.

A number of issues related to bilateral cooperation were also discussed. The two presidents noted mutual interest in countering the coronavirus, including collaboration in developing and producing vaccines. Specialized agencies will be instructed accordingly. The parties agreed to maintain regular contacts via diplomatic and military channels.

27 October 2020. The Russian President Vladimir Putin had a telephone conversation with President of the Republic of Turkey, Recep Tayyip Erdogan, at the initiative of the Turkish side.

The two presidents discussed in detail interaction on the Syrian track, stressing the importance of cooperation in implementing the existing agreements on stabilizing Idlib and the east bank of the Euphrates. The leaders also shared opinions on the issues of political settlement in Syria, including with support from the Astana process guarantor states. The Libyan agenda was also covered, including prospects for further normalization of the situation and stepping up intra-Libyan peace talks.

In addition, developments in the Nagorno-Karabakh conflict zone were discussed. The Russian side expressed deep concern over the ongoing hostilities and the increasing involvement of Middle East terrorists. Vladimir Putin informed his counterpart about his meetings with the leaders of Azerbaijan and Armenia, and the efforts to reach a ceasefire and deescalate the crisis as soon as possible. It was agreed to maintain coordination between Russian and Turkish foreign and defense ministries, as well as the two countries' special services.

Greece: (Population 11.1 M, rank 82, decrease 0.2%. Free: 84 of 100).

21 October 2020. UK Prime Minister Boris Johnson spoke with Prime Minister Mitsotakis of Greece.

They discussed their countries' respective efforts to fight coronavirus and agreed to work together to ensure a sustainable global recovery, including through the development of a vaccine.

The Prime Minister updated Prime Minister Mitsotakis on the UK's negotiations with the EU. He reaffirmed that the EU have effectively ended those negotiations by stating they did not want to change their negotiating position. Should the EU fundamentally change their position, then the UK would be willing to talk on that new basis.

The two leaders discussed the recent tensions in the Eastern Mediterranean. The Prime Minister stressed the need for dialogue and welcomed the public commitment from Greece to resolve differences with Turkey diplomatically. He confirmed the UK would continue to work with both sides to de-escalate the situation. The Prime Minister and Prime Minister Mitsotakis also reflected on the outcome of the recent Turkish Cypriot elections. The Prime Minister was clear that a settlement in Cyprus was in everyone's interest. Finally, the leaders resolved to continue to work together to enhance the UK-Greece relationship, particularly ahead of Greece's bicentenary in 2021.

Republic of North Macedonia: (Population 2 M, rank 147, growth 0.1%. Partly Free: 57 of 100).

Albania: (Population 2.9 M, rank 139, growth 0.1%. Partly free: 68 of 100).

Cyprus: (Population 1.1 M, rank 159, growth 0.8%. Free: 94 of 100.

Kazakhstan (Population 18.2 M, rank 64, growth 1.2%. Not free: 22 of 100. Area 2.72 M km^2, rank 9.).

Armenia: (Population 2.9 M, rank 138, growth 0.2%. Partly free: 45 of 100).

2 October 2020. Vladimir Putin had a telephone conversation with Prime Minister of the Republic of Armenia, Nikol Pashinyan, at the Armenian side's initiative.

The two leaders continued discussing the situation in the Nagorno-Karabakh conflict zone. They expressed serious concern over the incoming information on the involvement in hostilities of militants of illegal armed units from the Middle East.

Vladimir Putin again emphasized the need to immediately stop the hostilities and resume political and diplomatic efforts to settle the conflict in line with the Statement made by the presidents of the countries – co-chairs of the OSCE Minsk Group (Russia, France and the US) on October 1, 2020.

It was agreed to maintain contacts in different formats.

5 October 2020. Vladimir Putin had a telephone conversation with Prime Minister of Armenia Nikol Pashinyan at the initiative of the Armenian side.

The leaders continued their discussion of the escalating armed conflict in Nagorno-Karabakh, which has grown in scale and has seen serious losses on both sides, including among civilians.

Vladimir Putin again emphasized the urgent need for a ceasefire.

Azerbaijan: (Population 9.8 M, rank 90, growth 1.1%. Not free 14 of 100).

1 October 2020. Statement of the presidents of Russia, the United States and France on Nagorno-Karabakh.

The President of the Russian Federation Vladimir Putin, the President of the United States of America Donald Trump, and the President of the French Republic Emmanuel Macron, representing the Co-Chair countries of the OSCE Minsk Group, condemn in the strongest terms the recent escalation of violence along the Line of Contact in the Nagorno-Karabakh conflict zone.

We deplore the loss of human lives, and extend our condolences to the families of those killed and injured. We call for an immediate cessation of hostilities between the relevant military forces.

We also call on the leaders of Armenia and Azerbaijan to commit without delay to resuming substantive negotiations, in good faith and without preconditions, under the auspices of the OSCE Minsk Group Co-Chairs.

8 October 2020. Statement made by President of the Russian Federation Vladimir Putin:

"Having engaged in a series of telephone conversations with President of the Republic of Azerbaijan Ilham Aliyev and Prime Minister of the Republic of Armenia Nikol Pashinyan, the President of Russia calls for halting the hostilities in the Nagorno-Karabakh conflict zone on humanitarian grounds, in order to carry out an exchange of bodies of the deceased and prisoners.

The foreign ministers of Azerbaijan and Armenia are invited to Moscow on October 9 to hold consultations on these matters, mediated by the Russian Foreign Ministry."

Uzbekistan: (Population 31.9 M, rank 44, growth 1.5%. Not free: 3 of 100).

Kyrgyzstan (Population 6 M, rank 112, growth 1.5%. Partly free, 37 of 100).

Tajikistan: (Population 8.9 M, rank 96, growth 2.1%. Not free, 11 of 100).

Turkmenistan: (Population 5.7 M, rank 113, growth 1.7%. Not free, 4 of 100).

USA: The east side of the Highland Lighthouse, at 27 Highland Light Rd, North Truro, 10 km east of Provincetown, northeast of Cape Cod.

United Kingdom, Canada, South America

United Kingdom: (Population: 66.1 M, rank 21, growth 0.6%. Free: 95 of 100).

30 September 2020. UK prime Minister: And yesterday we saw the biggest rise in daily cases since the pandemic began, today a further 7,108. We've also had a tragic increase in the number of daily deaths – with 71 yesterday and again today.

Reports: All people would like to see UK a world-leader in building peace, freedom, health, harmony and prosperity for all.

7 October 2020. Prime Minister Boris Johnson spoke to the President of the European Council, Charles Michel.

The UK Prime Minister, Boris Johnson, and the President of the European Council, Charles Michel, spoke today to take stock of negotiations on the future relationship between the UK and the EU. The Prime Minister outlined our clear commitment to trying to reach an agreement, underlining that a deal was better for both sides. He also underlined that, nevertheless, the UK was prepared to end the transition period on Australia-style terms, if an agreement could not be found. Although some progress had been made in recent discussions, they acknowledged that significant areas of difference remain, particularly on fisheries. Chief Negotiators should continue to work intensively in the coming days to try to bridge the gaps.

The Prime Minister reiterated that any deal must reflect what the British people voted for, and that businesses and citizens needed certainty very soon on the terms of our future relationship.

They agreed to remain in touch on this issue.

12 October 2020. The PM informed about the stark reality of the second wave of this virus: the number of cases has quadrupled in the last three weeks, there are now more people in hospital with Covid-19 than when we went into lockdown on March 23, and deaths are already rising.

Ireland: (Population: 4.7 M, rank 123, growth 0.8%. Free: 96 of 100)

Canada: (Population: 36.6 M, rank 38, growth 0.9%. Free: 99 of 100. Area 9.9 M km², rank 2).

Iceland: (Population: 335,000, rank 180, growth 0.8%. Free 97 of 100).

Mexico: (Population: 129.1 M, rank 10, growth 1.3%. Partly Free: 65 of 100. Area 1.96 M km^2, rank 13).

Reports: Mexico maintains its position as the 15th largest economy in the world, and the second largest economy in Latin America, though it experienced no economic growth in 2019. The 2019 average exchange was $19.21 MXP, and Mexico imported $6.1 B in processed food products from the United States. Milk was the most imported, followed by beef and pork products. Likewise, Mexico exported $22.2 B in processed foods to the United States. The largest categories of exports to the United States were beer, avocados, tomatoes, chili peppers and beef. The key players in the HRI sector in Mexico are Alsea (18 casual eating brands), FEMSA – OXXO (19,558 convenience stores), CMR (12 brands), IHG (12 brands), Marriott International (14 brands), Hyatt Group (7 brands) and Hilton Hotels (7 brands).

Chile: (Population: 18 M, rank 65, growth 0.8%. Free 94 of 100).

Colombia: (Population: 49 M, rank 29, growth 0.8%. Partly free 64 of 100).

Argentina: (Population: 44.2 M, rank 31, growth, 1%. Free: 82 of 100. Area 2.78 M km^2, rank 8.).

Brazil (Population: 209.2 M, rank 6, growth 0.8%. Free, 79 of 100. Area 8.5 M km^2, rank 5).

Ecuador: (Population: 17.3 M, rank 67, growth 1.7%. Partly free: 57 of 100)

Peru: (Population: 32.1 M, rank 5, growth 1.2%. Free: 72 of 100)

Cuba: (Population: 11.4 M, rank 42, growth 0.1%. Not free, 15 of 100).

Bolivia: (Population: 11 M, rank 83, growth 1.5%. Partly free 68 of 100).

Paraguay: (Population: 6.8 M, rank 107, growth 1.3%. Partly free 64 of 100).

Panama: (Population: 4.1 M, rank 131, growth 1.6%. Free: 83 of 100).

Venezuela: (Population: 32 M, rank 43, growth 1.3%. Not free: 30 of 100).

Guyana: (Population 777K, (rank 165, growth 0.6%). Free: 74 of 100).

Trinidad and Tobago: (Population 1.3 M, (rank 153, growth 0.3%). Free: 81 of 100).

Nicaragua: (Population 6.2 M, (rank 110, growth 1.1%). Partly Free: 47 of 100).

El Salvador: (Population 6.3 M (rank 108, growth 0.5%). Free: 70 of 100).

Guatemala: (Population 17.6 M (rank 89, growth 1.93%). Partly Free: 52 of 100).

France, Germany, and neighbors

France: (Population 64.9 M, rank 22, growth 0.4%. Free: 90 of 100).

30 September 2020. The Russian President Vladimir Putin had a telephone conversation with President of the French Republic, Emmanuel Macron, at the initiative of the French side.

The presidents discussed the sharp escalation in the zone of the Nagorno-Karabakh conflict. They expressed deep concern over the continued large-scale hostilities there. Vladimir Putin and Emmanuel Macron called on the conflicting sides to fully cease fire without delay, deescalate tensions and show maximum restraint.

They pointed out that there is no alternative to a diplomatic and political settlement of the Nagorno-Karabakh crisis. In this context, they discussed the practical aspects of their further interaction, primarily within the OSCE Minsk Group. They expressed readiness to issue a statement on behalf of the Minsk Group co-chairs (Russia, France and the United States) regarding the immediate termination of the hostilities and the resumption of negotiations.

Vladimir Putin and Emmanuel Macron also spoke about the developments following the presidential election in Belarus. The Russian leader reaffirmed the position of principle that any interference in the internal affairs of the sovereign state and external pressure on the legitimate authorities are unacceptable.

It was agreed to maintain contact.

20 October 2020. Vladimir Putin had a telephone conversation with President of France Emmanuel Macron, at the French side's initiative.

The Russian President expressed his condolences in connection with the terrorist act – the barbaric murder of a French teacher – that took place in the Paris suburbs on October 16. In this context, mutual interest in stepping up cooperation to combat terrorism, and the spread of extremist ideology, was reaffirmed.

The presidents discussed in detail developments in the conflict zone around Nagorno-Karabakh. Vladimir Putin informed his counterpart about the steps being taken to prevent the further escalation of hostilities, and the prompt resumption of negotiations with a view to a political and diplomatic settlement of the Nagorno-Karabakh conflict. The importance of observing the ceasefire agreements by the parties to the conflict reached on October 10 and 17 was stressed. Interest in continuing close coordination between Russia and France as co-chairs of the OSCE Minsk Group, as well as through the UN Security Council, was emphasized.

It was agreed to maintain contact at various levels.

Belgium (Population 11.4 M, rank 80, growth 0.6%. Free: 95 of 100).

The Belgian biotech company Galapagos has had a difficult path to the market, with the EU and Japan embracing its rheumatoid arthritis drug shortly after the FDA did not approve it.

Reports: With COVID-19 cases surging in much of Europe, governments continue to impose greater measures aimed at curbing a second wave. Switzerland announced mask mandates and banned large-scale public gatherings, while Belgium tightened restrictions and curfews, with its health minister warning of a "coronavirus tsunami." Elsewhere, Italy approved fresh anti-coronavirus controls, Ireland was set to approve its tightest measures since April, and tougher U.K. lockdowns are likely coming to Wales and Manchester.

European Commission, European Union, EU: 27 EU countries: Austria, Belgium, Bulgaria, Croatia, Republic of Cyprus, Czech Republic, Denmark, Estonia, Finland, France, Germany, Greece, Hungary, Ireland, Italy, Latvia, Lithuania, Luxembourg, Malta, Netherlands, Poland, Portugal, Romania, Slovakia, Slovenia, Spain, and Sweden.

The **European Council** is made up of the heads of state or government of all EU countries, the European Council President, and the European Commission President.

NATO 29 member states: Albania, Belgium, Bulgaria, Canada, Croatia, Czech Republic, Denmark, Estonia, France, Germany, Greece, Hungary, Iceland, Italy, Latvia, Lithuania, Luxembourg, Montenegro, Netherlands, Norway, Poland, Portugal, Romania, Slovakia, Slovenia, Spain, Turkey, United Kingdom, and United States

NATO was created in 1949 with 12 states, and now includes 29 countries. The aggregate war-related expenses of its members exceed 70% of the world's total war-related spending.

Germany: (Population 82.1 M, rank 16, growth 0.2%. Free: 95 of 100).

Reports: Researchers at Helmholtz Zentrum München, and the Technical University of Munich (TUM), have developed the world's smallest ultrasound detector. Based on miniaturized photonic circuits on top of a silicon chip, it is 100 times smaller than an average human hair. The new detector can visualize features that are much smaller than previously possible, leading to what is known as super-resolution imaging.

Reports: With more than 83 millions of the world's wealthiest consumers, Germany is the largest market for food and agricultural products in the European Union. The German market offers good opportunities for U.S. exporters of consumer-oriented products, particularly nuts, fish and seafood products, dried fruits, sauces and condiments, bakery products, organic products, and sweet potatoes. In 2019, German food service sales increased by 11.9% to USD 110.8 B (triple the growth from previous year), with all three major market segments—hotel, restaurant, and catering/institutional—enjoying increased sales. Restaurants led the food service market in 2019, with USD 60 B in sales. Key trends include sustainability, regional produce, convenience, health and wellness, and retail catering. COVID-19 related lock-down and physical distancing measures heavily impacted the German food sector and consumers' shopping.

Reports: Germany posted its highest ever increase in confirmed COVID-19 cases over the past 24 hours and started reimposing restrictions on some of the biggest coronavirus hotspots such as Berlin. The French government meanwhile declared a public health state of emergency and announced a curfew for Paris and eight other big cities from Saturday17 Oct. Italy has also surpassed its daily record for newly diagnosed coronavirus cases, while a debate is taking place in England over whether a country-wide "circuit breaker" lockdown is needed.

On Wednesday, 28 Oct, Germany announced a four-week shutdown of restaurants, bars, cinemas and theaters, while France said it would impose a second national lockdown, as coronavirus infections surge across the region.

Norway (Population 5.3 M, rank 118, growth 1%. Free: 100 of 100).

Sweden (Population 9.9 M, rank 89, growth 0.7%. Free: 100 of 100).

The Swedish antibody developer BioInvent International has licensed its solid tumor and blood cancer drug to the US CASI Pharmaceuticals for development and commercialization in the Greater China region.

The Netherlands (Population 17 M, rank 67, growth 0.3%. Free: 99 of 100).

Reports: Wageningen Bioveterinary Research has identified the presence of highly pathogenic avian influenza (H5N8) (HPAI) in two dead swans. The two swans were part of a group of six that were found dead in the Netherlands, near Kockengen (in the province of Utrecht).

History: Four hundred years ago, in 1620, the Pilgrims arrived in Massachusetts on the Mayflower, after a long journey from Europe. Many of the Pilgrims actually started their journey in Leiden in the Netherlands, where they had lived for 12 years after leaving England as refugees. There is a 1620 painting of the Pilgrims departing the Netherlands, by Adam Willaerts, *The Departure of the Pilgrims from Delftshaven*, 1620.

While CAR T-cell therapies have changed the face of cancer treatment, the necessity to personalize them to each patient makes the logistics of the therapy difficult. The Dutch company Kiadis Pharma aims to overcome this obstacle by sourcing cancer therapies cheaply and quickly from donors, based on a type of immune cell called natural killer cells.

Czech Republic (Population 10.6 M, rank 87, growth 0.1%. Free: 94 of 100).

Denmark (Population 5.7 M, rank 114, growth 0.4%. Free: 97 of 100. Area (including Greenland) 2.22 M km^2, rank 12 but not official).

Reports: Denmark is the world's largest producer of mink skins. The country began instituting a series of protective measures in the summer of 2020 to limit the spread of coronavirus (COVID-19) on Danish mink farms, but outbreaks have persisted, and it was an increase in cases in late September.

Luxembourg (Population 583 K, rank 169, growth 1.3%. Free: 98 of 100).

Spain: (Population 46.3 M, rank 30, growth 0%. Free: 94 of 100).

Reports: Spain received 72.4% less tourists during the first seven months of 2020, compared to the previous year. Following seven weeks of strict confinement, gathering restrictions, and capacity limits inside restaurants across the country, the Spanish hospitality sector estimates that about 40,000 businesses have already closed. Under the current scenario, the sector expects a total of 65,000 establishments will disappear by the end of the year.

Portugal: (Population 10.3 M, rank 88, decrease 0.4%. Free: 97 of 100).

Liechtenstein: (Population: 38,000, rank 215, growth 0.7%, Free: 91 of 100)

Andorra: (Population: 77,100, rank 203, growth 0.18%, Free: 94 of 100)

The IMF welcomed the Principality of Andorra as its 190th member this month.

India, Pakistan, Australia, and neighbors

India (Population: 1.3 B, rank 2nd, growth 1.1%. Free: 77 of 100. Area 3.28 M km^2, rank 7).

Indonesia: (Population: 263.9 M, rank 4, growth 1.1%. Partly free: 65 of 100. Area 1.91 M km^2, rank 14.).

Australia: (Population: 24.4 M, rank 53, growth 1.3%. Free: 98 of 100. Area 7.69 M km^2, rank 6).

New Zealand: (Population 4.7 M, rank 125, growth 1%. Free: 98 of 100.

Pakistan: (Population 212 M, rank 5, growth 2%. Partly free: 43 of 100).

Philippines: (Population 104.9 M, rank 13, growth 1.5%. Partly free 63 of 100).

Singapore: (Population 5.7 M, rank 115, growth 1.5%. Partly free 51 of 100).

The EAS currently comprises 18 countries: 10 ASEAN members (Brunei Darussalam, Cambodia, Indonesia, Laos, Malaysia, Myanmar, the Philippines, Singapore, Thailand and Vietnam), and eight dialogue partners: Russia (joined the EAS in 2010), the United States, Japan, South Korea, India, China, Australia and New Zealand.

APEC (21 members: Singapore, China, USA, Vietnam, Australia, Japan, Indonesia, Russia, Philippines, Malaysia, Hong Kong, Thailand, Chile, Canada, New Zealand, South Korea, Peru, Mexico, Brunei, Papua New Guinea, Chinese Taipei)

Thailand: (Population 69 M, rank 20, growth 0.3%. Not free 32 of 100).

Reports: Bank of Thailand launches world's first government savings bond on IBM blockchain technology.

Myanmar (Burma, Population 53.3 M, rank 26, growth 0.9%. Not free 32 of 100.

Bangladesh (Population 164.6 M, rank 8, growth 1.1%. Partly free 47 of 100).

Sri Lanka (Population 20.8 M, rank 58, growth 0.4%. Partly free 56 of 100).

Malaysia (Population 31.6 M, rank 45, growth 1.34%. Partly free 44 of 100).

Brunei: (Population 428,000, rank 176, growth 1.3%. Not free 29 of 100).

Vanuatu: (Population 276,000, rank 185, growth 2.2%. Free 80 of 100)

Tonga: (Population 108,000, rank 195, growth 0.8%. Free 74 of 100

Papua New Guinea: (Population 8.2 M, rank 101, growth 2.1%, Partly Free 64 of 100).

Italy, Middle East, Africa

Italy: (Population 59.3 M, rank 23, decrease 0.1%. Free: 89 of 100).

Vatican: (Population 792, rank 233 (last), decrease 1.1%).

San Marino: (Population 33,400, rank 218, growth 0.6%. Free 97 of 100)

Malta (Population 431,000, rank 175, growth 0.3%. Free, 96 of 100).

Jordan (Population 9.7 M, rank 92, growth 2.6%. Partly free, 37 of 100).

Lebanon: (Population: 6 M, rank 111, growth 1.3%. Partly free: 44 of 100).

United Arab Emirates (UAE) (Population: 9.4 M, rank 94, growth 1.4%. Not free, 20 of 100. Capital: Abu Dhabi. Big city: Dubai).

Saudi Arabia (Population 32.9 M, rank 41, growth 2.1%. Not free: 10 of 100. Area 2.149 M km^2, rank 12.).

13 October 2020. Vladimir Putin had a telephone conversation with Crown Prince of the Kingdom of Saudi Arabia, Mohammed bin Salman Al Saud, at the latter's initiative.

The sides positively assessed the level of bilateral relations and expressed mutual intention to further develop Russian-Saudi cooperation in various areas.

They exchanged in detail their views on the current situation in the world energy market, and emphasized the importance of continuing joint work, including in the OPEC Plus format.

17 October 2020. Vladimir Putin had a telephone conversation with Crown Prince of the Kingdom of Saudi Arabia Mohammed bin Salman Al Saud.

In follow-up to the previous telephone conversation, the parties had a detailed exchange of opinions on the progress of the existing OPEK Plus agreements. Both sides stressed again their readiness to continue close coordination in this area in the interests of maintaining stability in the global fuel market.

In addition, they discussed issues related to interaction in fighting the spread of the coronavirus infection, in particular, prospects for using the Russian Sputnik V vaccine in Saudi Arabia.

The parties pledged to continue contacts at different levels.

Yemen (Population 28.2 M, rank 50, growth 2.4%. Not free: 14 of 100).

Iraq (Population 38.2 M, rank 36, growth 2.9%. Not free: 27 of 100).

7 October 2020. EBRD shareholders approve membership of Iraq.

Iran: (Population 81.1 M, rank 18, growth 1.1%. Not free: 17 of 100).

10 October 2020. Vladimir Putin had a telephone conversation with President of the Islamic Republic of Iran, Hassan Rouhani, at the Iranian side's initiative.

The presidents had an extensive exchange of opinions on the developments in the Nagorno-Karabakh conflict zone. Vladimir Putin informed his Iranian counterpart about the efforts currently underway with Russia's mediation to de-escalate the tensions in the region. The President of Iran expressed support for the agreement reached following the trilateral consultations by the foreign ministers of Russia, Azerbaijan and Armenia on a ceasefire for humanitarian reasons as well as on the launch of substantive talks aimed at reaching a prompt peaceful settlement.

The two leaders also considered the developments around the Joint Comprehensive Plan of Action, and noted the importance of preserving this international agreement, which is essential for international security. Mr Putin and Mr Rouhani discussed current issues of bilateral trade and economic cooperation. They emphasized problems related to tackling the COVID-19 pandemic, paying particular attention to the prospects of interaction regarding the Russian-produced Sputnik V vaccine.

During the conversation, Mr Rouhani extended his warm wishes to Mr Putin in connection with his recent birthday.

The sides agreed on further contacts.

Israel: (Population 8.3 M, rank 100, growth 1.6%. Free: 80 of 100).

Reports: Israel is a net importer of all major categories of food products. Israeli food prices are 19% higher than the OECD average. Israeli citizens spend more than 16% of their income on food and beverages. In general, consumers choose to shop at supermarkets over traditional markets, due to competitive prices and longer hours of operation. Over 60% of consumers buy their food at supermarkets.

Palestine: (Population 4.9 M (rank 121, grows 2.7%). Not free: 28 of 100).

Egypt (Population 97.5 M (rank 14, grows 1.9%). Not free, 26 of 100).

League of Arab States (LAS) (22 countries: Algeria, Bahrein, Comoros, Djibouti, Egypt, Iraq, Jordan, Kuwait, Lebanon, Libya, Mauritania, Morocco, Oman, Palestine, Qatar, Saudi Arabia, Somalia, Sudan, Syria, Tunisia, United Arab Emirates and Yemen).

Qatar: (Population 2.6 M (rank 142, grows 2.7%). Not free: 26 of 100).

Kuwait: (Population 4.1 M (rank 130, grows 2.1%). Partly free: 36 of 100).

2 October 2020. Vladimir Putin sent greetings to Emir of the State of Kuwait, Sheikh Nawaf Al-Ahmad Al-Jaber Al-Sabah on his accession to the throne.

Vladimir Putin noted that Russia and Kuwait enjoy friendly, constructive relations, and confirmed his intention to continue joint work on developing bilateral cooperation in different areas as well as partnership in international affairs. "Undoubtedly, this serves the interests of the two nations and is in line with strengthening peace and security in the Middle East," the President stressed.

Oman: (Population 4.6 M (rank 127, grows 4.8%). Not free: 25 of 100)

Bahrain: (Population 1.5 M (rank 152, grows 4.7%). Not free: 12 of 100).

Syria: (Population 18.2 M (rank 63, decrease 0.9%). Not free: 0 of 100).

Kenya: (Population 49.7 M (rank 28, growth 2.6%. Partly free, 51 of 100).

Libya: (Population 6.3 M, rank 109, growth 1.3%. Not free: 13 of 100).

Algeria: (Population 41.3 M, rank 34, growth 1.8%. Partly Free 35 of 100. Area 2.38 M km^2, rank 10.)

Tunisia: (Population 11.5 M, rank 78, growth 1.1%. Free: 78 of 100).

Morocco: (Population 35.7 M, rank 39, growth 1.3%. Partly free: 41 of 100).

South Africa: (Population 56.7 M, rank 25, growth 1.3%. Free, 78 of 100).

Zimbabwe: (Population 16.5 M, rank 70, growth 2.4%. Partly Free, 32 of 100).

Sudan (Population 40.5 M, rank 35, growth 2.4%. Not Free: 6 of 100).

South Sudan (Population 12.5 M, rank 76, growth 2.8%. Not Free: 4 of 100)

Guinea: (Population 12.7 M, rank 75, growth 2.6%. Partly Free, 41 of 100).

Djibouti (Population 957,000, rank 160, growth 1.6%. Not Free: 26 of 100).

Somalia: (Population 14.7 M, rank 74, growth 3%. Not free: 5 of 100).

Niger (Population 21.4 M, rank 57, growth 3.9%. Partly free: 49 of 100).

Nigeria (Population 190.8 M, rank 7, growth 2.6%. Partly free: 50 of 100).

Cameroon (Population 24 M, rank 55, growth 2.6%. Not free: 24 of 100).

Sierra Leone: (Population 7.5 M (rank 103, grows 2.2%). Partly free: 66 of 100)

Chad: (Population 15 M (rank 73, grows 3.1%). Not free: 18 of 100).

The Gambia: (Population 2.1 M (rank 146, grows 3%). Not free: 20 of 100).

Malawi: (Population 18.6 M (rank 61, grows 2.9%). Partly free: 63 of 100).

Rwanda: (Population 12.2 M (rank 77, grows 2.4%). Not free: 24 of 100).

Burkina Faso: (Population 19.1 M (rank 60, grows 2.9%). Partly free: 63 of 100).

Central African Republic: (Population 4.6 M (rank 126, grows 1.4%). Not free: 10 of 100).

Senegal: (Population 15.8 M (rank 72, grows 2.8%). Free: 78 of 100).

Gabon: (Population 2 M (rank 149, grows 2.3%). Partly Free: 32 of 100).

Madagascar: (Population 25.5 M (rank 51, grows 2.7%). Partly Free: 56 of 100).

Democratic Republic of the Congo: (Population 81.3 M (rank 17, grows 3.3%). Not Free: 19 of 100. Area 2.34 M km^2, rank 11).

Angola: (Population 29.7 M (rank 46, grows 3.4%). Not Free: 24 of 100).

Zambia: (Population 17 M (rank 66, grows 3%). Partly Free: 56 of 100).

United Republic of Tanzania: (Population 57 M (rank 24, grows 3.1%). Partly Free: 58 of 100).

Ethiopia: (Population 105 M (rank 12, grows 2.5%). Not Free: 12 of 100).

Uganda: (Population 42.8 M (rank 33, grows 3.3%). Partly Free: 35 of 100).

Mozambique: (Population 30.3 M (rank 46, grows 2.9%). Partly Free: 53 of 100).

Namibia: (Population 2.5 M (rank 143, grows 1.9%). Free: 77 of 100).

Mauritius: (Population 1.2 M (rank 157, growth 0.8%). Free: 89 of 100).

Equatorial Guinea: (Population 1.35 M (rank 154, growth 3.6%). Not Free: 8 of 100).

Ghana: (Population 28.8 M (rank 48, growth 2.22%). Free: 83 of 100).

Côte d'Ivoire: (Population 25.7 M (rank 106, growth 2.58%). Partly Free: 51 of 100).

Italy, Rome, from Altare della Patria (with two pigeons): Forum Caesaris (center left, 46 BC, by Julius Caesar (100 – 44 BC), 160 m by 75 m, with Temple of Venus Genetrix (left down)), Via dei Fori Imperiali (center left), Forum Augustus (left, 2 BC).

Medical

Reports: As of September 2020, the Americas region has the highest number of health care workers infected in the world, with at least 570 000, and more than 2,500 have fallen – and still counting. With the region accounting for half of the world's COVID 19 cases, the scale of this pandemic is unprecedented.

Researchers have found a way to send tiny, soft robots into humans, potentially opening the door for less invasive surgeries, and ways to deliver treatments for conditions ranging from colon polyps and stomach cancer, to aortic artery blockages.

Researchers in the Department of Biomedical Engineering at Texas A&M University are working on a new way to detect blood clots. The device could be used to design and monitor drugs for patients suffering from clotting disorders.

Researchers at the University of Houston report that they have designed and produced a smart electronic skin, and a medical robotic hand, capable of assessing vital diagnostic data, by using a newly invented rubbery semiconductor with high carrier mobility.

Reports: Commenting at a Financial Times conference, Moderna CEO Stéphane Bancel stated the company will not be able to apply for emergency use authorization in the U.S. for COVID-19 vaccine mRNA-1273 before November 25 at the earliest. That reflects the minimum amount of time needed to accumulate enough safety data. He also said that the company does not expect full approval to distribute the vaccine to all sections of the U.S. population until next spring.

MeiraGTx presented nine-month results from the ongoing Phase 1/2 clinical trial of AAV-RPGR for vision loss at an oral session at the EURETINA 2020 Virtual Meeting, October 2-4.

Spring Bank Pharmaceuticals presented abstracts related to its IV SB 11285 Phase 1a/1b trial at the 7th ImmunoTherapy of Cancer (ITOC7) conference from October 3-5.

Alexion Pharmaceuticals presented on its strategic advancement, including key pipeline opportunities and drivers of future growth at an event on October 6. Also on October 11 FDA decided on a new formulation of Alexion's Ultomiris that will shorten infusion time.

White blood cells are part the immune system, and help the body fight off infections and other diseases.

5 October 2020. The Nobel Assembly at Karolinska Institutet has today decided to award the 2020 Nobel Prize in Physiology or Medicine jointly to Harvey J. Alter, Michael Houghton and Charles M. Rice for the discovery of Hepatitis C virus.

Harvey J. Alter was born in 1935 in New York. He received his medical degree at the University of Rochester Medical School, and trained in internal medicine at Strong Memorial Hospital and at the University Hospitals of Seattle. In 1961, he joined the National Institutes of Health (NIH) as a clinical associate. He spent several years at Georgetown University before returning to NIH in 1969 to join the Clinical Center's Department of Transfusion Medicine as a senior investigator.

Michael Houghton was born in the United Kingdom. He received his PhD degree in 1977 from King's College London. He joined G. D. Searle & Company before moving to Chiron Corporation, Emeryville, California in 1982. He relocated to University of Alberta in 2010 and is currently a Canada Excellence Research Chair in Virology and the Li Ka Shing Professor of Virology at the University of Alberta where he is also Director of the Li Ka Shing Applied Virology Institute.

Charles M. Rice was born in 1952 in Sacramento. He received his PhD degree in 1981 from the California Institute of Technology where he also trained as a postdoctoral fellow between 1981-1985. He established his research group at Washington University School of Medicine, St Louis in 1986 and became full Professor in 1995. Since 2001 he has been Professor at the Rockefeller University,

New York. During 2001-2018 he was the Scientific and Executive Director, Center for the Study of Hepatitis C at Rockefeller University where he remains active.

A special committee, formed at the behest of the CDC and NIH, recommends a four-phase deployment of COVID-19 vaccines, after emergency use authorization (EUA), likely to happen later this quarter, that prioritizes vulnerable populations. First up would be front-line healthcare workers and first responders. The federal officials, who expect to ship initial doses within 24 hours of EUA, agree also with another of the committee's suggestions - no out-of-pocket costs for vaccination.

A carbohydrate called heparan sulfate, which is found on cell surfaces, may play a critical role in the new coronavirus' ability to infect cells.

Reports: Researchers study which cognitive operations underpin a given conscious perception. Neuroscientists track the neural correlates of consciousness in the brain, the organ of the mind. Programmable computers will not have consciousness. Even a perfect software model of the brain is not conscious. Consciousness is about being.

Reports: NIH clinical trial testing hyperimmune intravenous immunoglobulin plus remdesivir to treat COVID-19 begins - the study is taking place in hospitalized adults in the United States, Mexico and 16 other countries.

A new rapid test has been developed for the Bosch Vivalytic analysis device that detects the SARS-CoV-2 pathogen. The test provides a reliable result in 39 minutes, and is currently the fastest polymerase chain reaction (PCR) test worldwide.

Scientists have demonstrated a quick and effective mass testing approach using saliva samples to detect individuals who have been infected with COVID-19, but are still not showing symptoms.

Regeneron Pharmaceuticals has asked the Food and Drug Administration to provide emergency use authorization to its REGN-COV2 investigational antibody combination for COVID-19. The company says it currently has enough doses for about 50,000 patients, and expects to have enough for 300,000 patients within the next few months.

Neuromodulation, where devices control the firing of nerve cells, has been in use for decades to treat conditions such as Parkinson's disease and chronic pain. There are companies developing devices to treat sleep disorders, migraine headaches, and more.

Bristol Myers Squibb is hosting an event to discuss results from the Phase 3 True North trial evaluating Zeposia (ozanimod, which will be presented at United European Gastroenterology Week 2020).

The 2020 Virtual Cell & Gene Meeting on the Mesa event included on-demand presentations from Applied Genetic Technologies, Passage Bio, Caladrius Biosciences, Gamida Cell, Iovance Biotherapeutics, Generation Bio, and Genprex.

NIH: Finding from ABCD Study elucidates neural mechanisms that may underlie early weight gain.

A team at Vanderbilt University developed a back-assist exosuit.

University of Missouri researchers are creating pencil-drawn sensors. The engineers demonstrated that the simple combination of pencils and paper could be used to create personal, health-monitoring devices. Pencil-drawn graphite patterns serve as conductive traces and sensing electrodes, and office-copy papers work as flexible supporting substrates. The enabled devices can then perform real-time, continuous, and high-fidelity monitoring of a range of vital biophysical and biochemical signals from human bodies, including skin temperatures, heart rates, and sweat.

The Great Barrington Declaration was organized by infectious-disease experts Dr. Martin Kulldorff of Harvard University, Dr. Sunetra Gupta of Oxford University, and Dr. Jay Bhattacharya of Stanford University, and recommends allowing people to live normally despite the virus, while protecting the most vulnerable people, in order to avoid the lockdowns' devastating physical, mental, economic, and educational impacts. To date over 5,500 medical and public health scientists, and 11,000 medical practitioners have signed it. That numbers continue to grow. The Declaration expresses "grave concerns about the damaging physical and mental health impacts of the prevailing COVID-19 policies," pointing out that the "heaviest burden" is falling on "working-class and younger members of society." According to the Declaration, "[c]urrent lockdown policies are producing devastating effects on short and long-term public health." It concludes that "[k]eeping these measures in place until a vaccine is available will cause irreparable damage, with the underprivileged disproportionately harmed."

The study of Johnson & Johnson's COVID-19 vaccine has been temporarily stopped due to an unexplained illness in a trial participant, according to a report by health care news provider STAT. Clinical trial pauses are not uncommon, and in some cases last only a few days; study pauses also are not surprising given the size of Johnson & Johnson's 60 K-patient clinical trial. News of the halt comes after AstraZeneca also paused tests of its vaccine after a trial participant fell ill; the study has resumed in some countries but remains halted in the U.S.

A 25-year-old man, who is a resident of Washoe County in Nevada, became seriously ill following a second infection with COVID-19, a study in the *Lancet Infectious Diseases* journal showed, raising further questions about coronavirus immunity. A comparison of genetic codes showed "significant differences" between each virus variant, meaning the patient caught the coronavirus on two separate occasions, rather than the original infection bouncing back after becoming dormant. Reports of secondary coronavirus infections in Hong Kong, the Netherlands and Belgium were no more serious than the first, but one in Ecuador was similar to the U.S. case in being more severe.

The anatomy of the human ear makes it difficult to deliver medications to treat inner-ear conditions. The added manufactured microneedles will help. The National Institute on Deafness and Other Communication Disorders (NIDCD) is helping.

A single hair has a normal life between 2 and 7 years. Then it falls out and is replaced with a new hair, but, at old age, the rate of hair growth slows down.

About 65 millions of Americans are affected by digestive diseases.

Most autoimmune therapies aim to tune-down, regulate or re-polarize the T-cell response. Contrarily, immuno-oncology strategies attempt to mobilize anti-tumor response or not to stop an existing T-cell response.

The FDA decided on Zosano Pharma's Qtypyta on October 20.

The Prostate Cancer Foundation Scientific Retreat on October 23 will include presentations on Phase 1 data from Fortress Biotech and Mustang Bio on MB-105.

Portable sequencing is making it possible for geneticists to bring the lab to the field.

A new project will explore how artificial muscles could radically transform treatment options in the future. emPOWER robotic muscles will be implanted to replace the body's damaged or aging muscles.

Leveraging robotics to automate medical device manufacturing enables companies to improve processes, increase efficiencies, reduce defects, and reduce the frequency of in-process inspections.

Noise is all around you, from headphones and televisions to lawnmowers and washing machines. But sounds that are too loud, or loud sounds over a long period of time, can damage sensitive structures of the inner ear and cause noise-induced hearing loss.

Sound is measured in units called decibels. Sounds at or below 70 A-weighted decibels (dBA) are generally safe. Here are some decibel ratings for common sounds:

Normal conversation: 60-70 dBA

Lawnmowers: 80 to 100 dBA

Sports events: 94 to 110 dBA

Sirens from emergency vehicles: 110 to 129 dBA

Fireworks: 140 to 160 dBA

SQI and McMaster University seek to measure severity of COVID-19 - both have created a surface that repels every other element of human blood except critical cytokine biomarkers, like Interleukin-6, enabling timely and clear detection of critical "cytokine storm" progress of COVID-19 in individual patients.

Conjunctivitis, also called pinkeye, can happen in a smaller number of COVID-19 cases.

Until last year, there was no approved treatment for the rare autoimmune condition neuromyelitis optica. However, three antibody drugs have emerged in the last year, and Chord Therapeutics could lead to a small molecule drug for the condition, that doesn't require injecting, as the current treatments do.

The combination of advanced sequencing technologies, and user-friendly data analysis techniques, is bringing metagenomics into the reach of more scientists, creating new opportunities to ask and answer important research questions.

Kala Pharmaceuticals' Eysuvis (loteprednol etabonate ophthalmic suspension) 0.25% for dry eye is ready for approval.

The Allogeneic Cell Therapies Summit 2020 (October 26-28) has presentations from Adicet Bio, Allogene Therapeutics, Atara Biotherapeutics, bluebird bio, Precision Biosciences, Eli Lilly and TCR2 Therapeutics.

AI-powered polyp detector shown to find unremarkable colorectal lesions - discovery, developed by Pentax Medical and available in Europe, supports endoscopists in locating lesions they might otherwise miss, due to fatigue or distraction.

Sensor rapidly detects COVID-19 infection status, severity, immunity - a new type of multiplexed test with a low-cost sensor may enable the at-home diagnosis of a COVID infection through rapid analysis of small volumes of saliva or blood, without the involvement of a medical professional, in less than 10 minutes.

Skin-like wearable sensor helps ALS patients communicate.

Bayer is paying as much as $4 B for U.S. biotech firm Asklepios BioPharmaceutical. The latest deal, which includes upfront consideration of $2 B and potential milestone payments of up to $2 B, is related to the cutting-edge gene therapy, which offers the potential to cure a wide range of often-rare diseases by editing errors in the body's instruction manual. Drugmakers including Novartis, Roche Holding and Bristol-Myers Squibb have also interest in the industry.

The COVID-19 vaccine being developed by the University of Oxford and AstraZeneca produces a robust antibody and T-cell immune response in elderly people, the group at highest risk, FT reports. While details of the finding are expected to be published shortly in a clinical journal, sources cautioned that positive immunogenicity tests do not guarantee that the vaccine will ultimately prove safe and effective in older people. AstraZeneca resumed the U.S. trial of its experimental vaccine on Friday, 23 Oct, after a pause due to safety concerns, while Johnson & Johnson also restarted trials, saying the first batches of its shot could be available in January 2021.

Eli Lilly ends COVID-19 antibody trial after lack of improvement.

Universal flu vaccines could offer a way to protect against all the seasonal flu strains.

Antibody-drug conjugates (ADCs) offer a way to deliver powerful chemotherapies with fewer side effects than the chemotherapy alone.

Over 4% of the world's population suffers from one or more of over 80 autoimmune diseases identified to date. A large variety of treatment approaches has already been developed to curb the detrimental effects of autoimmune diseases.

Italy, Roma, Trajan's Market (113 AD, left), Augustus' Forum (12 AD, center), and policemen on horses.

Mathematics, Science, Technology, AI, Space

Robots usually only rely on vision and increasingly, touch. Researchers found that robot perception could improve markedly by adding hearing. Hearing also could help robots determine what type of action caused a sound and help them use sounds to predict the physical properties of new objects.

A method was developed for mass-producing tiny robots no bigger than a cell. The microscopic devices might eventually be used to monitor conditions inside an oil or gas pipeline, or to search out disease while floating through the bloodstream.

Always mathematical formulae and structures are a sine qua non requirement for formulating all physical and nature's laws.

Specialists make bioplastics based on a polymer called polylactic acid (PLA), which allows plastics to be biodegradable.

A Purdue University research team is working on inventions to use micro-chip technology in implantable devices and other wearable products to improve biomedical devices, including those used to monitor glaucoma and heart disease.

The proliferation and miniaturization of electronics in devices, wearables, medical implants, and other applications, has made technologies for blocking electromagnetic interference (EMI) especially important. However, traditional EMI shields need to be very thick to be effective. One solution could be MXenes, a family of 2D transition metal carbides, nitrides, and carbonitrides that demonstrate high conductivity and excellent EMI shielding properties.

Nvidia hosted its GPU Technology Conference from October 5-9. The event was continuously across all time zones for five days, and covered all the latest innovations from the company.

Nvidia has a longer-term vision in "all-pervasive AI/accelerated computing". NVIDIA has its AI Center of Excellence in the UK.

An array of 960 microphones placed off the end of a runway were used by NASA to record the sound of a low-flying Boeing 787-10 Dreamliner passing overhead. NASA is studying how aircraft noise changes based on the placement of the jet engines in relation to the main airframe and wing.

Engineers at MIT and the University of Massachusetts at Lowell designed the first completely flat fisheye lens to produce crisp, 180-degree panoramic images. The lenses, according to researchers, could someday be integrated into medical imaging devices, such as endoscopes, as well as in virtual reality glasses, wearable electronics, and other computer vision devices.

Using artificial intelligence and MRI scans, researchers identified signs of osteoarthritis three years before diagnosis.

Computer-designed proteins may protect against coronavirus.

A new lab-on-a-chip can help study tumor heterogeneity to reduce resistance to cancer therapies. The researchers combined artificial intelligence, microfluidics, and nanoparticle inkjet printing in a device that enables the examination and differentiation of cancers and healthy tissues at the single-cell level.

Engineers have invented a way to spray extremely thin wires made of a plant-based material that could be used to improve N95 mask filters. The spray could also potentially be used in the creation of human organs. The method involves spraying methylcellulose, a renewable plastic material derived from plant cellulose, onto added manufacturing objects.

Researchers design materials at the smallest scale, using single atoms to enable the rise to quantum technologies

Engineers work on new designs to develop compact underground electrical substations for urban areas.

The great mathematician Euler was featured on the sixth series of the Swiss 10-franc banknote, and on numerous Swiss, German, and Russian postage stamps. The asteroid 2002 Euler was named in his honor.

Euler is the only mathematician to have *two* numbers named after him: the important Euler's number in calculus, e, approximately equal to 2.71828, and the Euler–Mascheroni constant γ (gamma) sometimes referred to as just "Euler's constant", approximately equal to 0.57721. It is not known whether γ is rational or irrational.

Euler introduced and popularized several notational conventions through his numerous and widely circulated textbooks. Most notably, he introduced the concept of a function and was the first to write $f(x)$ to denote the function f applied to the argument x. He also introduced the modern notation for the trigonometric functions, the letter e for the base of the natural logarithm (now also known as Euler's number), the Greek letter Σ for summations and the letter i to denote the imaginary unit. The use of the Greek letter π to denote the ratio of a circle's circumference to its diameter was also popularized by Euler, although it originated with the mathematician William Jones.

There ia a new technology that is transforming the capability of robots, from new capabilities in motors, miniaturization, vision systems, electronic components, and sensors.

A Purdue University team has created a mobile charging system for automated underwater vehicles, enabling the AUVs to perform longer tasks without the need for human intervention.

To keep their systems from overheating, University of Central Florida researchers are developing a way for large machines to "breathe" in and out.

University of Michigan engineers reported that their new self-erasing chips could help stop counterfeit electronics or provide alerts if sensitive shipments are tampered with. The chips use a new material that temporarily stores energy, changing the color of the light it emits. The self-erase period takes seven days, or users can delete on demand with a flash of blue light.

NASA selects Nokia to build first ever cellular network on the Moon.

An origami-inspired miniature robot moves in multiple dimensions to help correct hand tremors, and other disturbances during teleoperation. The robot is the size of a tennis ball, weighs about as much as a penny, and successfully performed a difficult mock surgical task.

A new robotic system may help hospitals preserve protective gear, limit staff exposure to COVID-19, and provide more time for clinical work. The robotic system gives medical staff the ability to remotely operate ventilators and other bedside machines from outside intensive care rooms of patients with infectious diseases.

Machine learning, deep learning, and artificial intelligence technology promises to help many areas, including IT security operations.

Aidoc received approval for an AI technique that flags incidental pulmonary embolism.

Size, weight, power consumption, and cooling technologies today block quantum computing from the embedded world, but new generations should yield advances in artificial intelligence and computer security.

New orchestration software lets people remotely connect to their unit operations, and provides centralized monitoring and visualization of their bioprocesses.

More companies are investing in edge computing.

A new wave of easy-to-use robot vision systems allows companies with no automation experience to enjoy the benefits of vision-powered production.

Fluoride materials are considered for extra-thin computer chips.

A new device made from perovskite — one of a large family of materials defined by their special crystal structure — can be directed in two directions: it can receive optical signals, and just as easily transmit them. This means that text and photographs can be wirelessly transmitted from one unit to the other and back again, using two identical units, and can be done in real time.

Metal halide perovskites offer numerous advantages, such as a tunable bandgap, and cost-effective fabrication processes, making them optimal material for solar-cell applications.

Engineers at the University of California San Diego have built a squid-like robot that can swim untethered, propelling itself by generating jets of water.

High-performance embedded computing is earning the benefits of open-systems standards, new FPGA architectures, and artificial intelligence for superior edge computing performance.

Lawrence Livermore National Laboratory (LLNL) has installed a state-of-the-art artificial intelligence (AI) accelerator from SambaNova Systems, the National Nuclear Security Administration (NNSA) announced Monday, 26 Oct, allowing researchers to more effectively combine AI and machine learning (ML) with complex scientific workloads. LLNL has begun integrating the new AI hardware, SambaNova Systems DataScale, into the NNSA's Corona supercomputing.

Controlling non-obvious variables using predictive analytics is very useful - predictive analytics through real-time, quantitative surface quality measurements, give manufacturers useful data. This monitors machine health and results in measurable cost reductions.

NASA's DuAxel rover – made of a pair of two-wheeled rovers, each called Axel – can lower its chassis and anchor to the ground before splitting in two. With the rear half firmly in place, the forward half undocks and rolls away on a single axle.

France, Lyon (43 BC, by Munatius Plancus (87 BC – 15 BC) and Lepidus (77 BC – 11 BC), lieutenants of Julius Caesar (100 BC – 44 BC)), part of eastern façade of the Hôtel de Ville (1645 – 1651, 1674) de Lyon, in Place de la Comédie, across Opéra.

General news and issues

October is Cyber Security Awareness Month.

The Covid-19 pandemic has been accompanied by a surge of cyberattacks in the life sciences industry.

Financial services industry is one of the top targets for cyberattacks, with cybercriminals eager to steal highly valuable personal data to sell on the Dark Net. But they don't stop there. Any company that stores personal data is a target.

People ask authorities to arrest the cybercriminals.

Reports: In totalitarian systems there are quotas against different groups of people, for political reasons – now such quotas are also applied in some parts of the U.S.

Reports: Another outage hits Microsoft, as Outlook goes down worldwide.

Reports: Some sick people pay for bad ads, and other sick people accept those bad ads, both contributing to the mental intoxication of people – this will change soon, under the new World Constitution.

The Deutsche Bank dbAccess 28th Annual Leveraged Finance Conference 2020: Hilton Worldwide, Netflix, United Airlines.

NextEra Energy is the world's biggest provider of wind and solar energy.

Cryptocurrencies in general are called detrimental to the safety and stability of the international financial system due to the opportunities for rogue nations, criminals and terrorists to skirt reporting requirements.

Not responding – this is what people often receive from their software on computers.

There are companies which are very insulting and toxic for their customers – they will shortly disappear.

Reports: Virgin Galactic has confirmed that it is on track to conduct its first suborbital spaceflight in the coming weeks from Spaceport America in New Mexico. The flight planning window opens on October 22, and will be the first of two missions that will complete testing of the SpaceShipTwo spacecraft system. If both flights succeed, Virgin Galactic expects to fly founder Sir Richard Branson in the first quarter of 2021, notching a milestone that will commence the company's commercial tourism service.

Amazon will hire 100,000 seasonal workers for holidays.

USA, Boston: 3 Dec 2009, from Harvard Medical School looking northeast to the Avenue Louis Pasteur (1822-1895, French microbiologist),

Aphorisms

People are upset that the arrogance of power is still outrageous, but this will change soon.

All people want to embrace the world.

All people want to be healthy, not under the stress and anxiety of having a war.

Incompetence and arrogance are expanding.

The press of conformity is widespread.

France, Paris, the north-west part of L'Institut de France (1795, moved in 1805 by Napoléon in this baroque building from 1684) is a revered French cultural society with five académies, the most famous being Académie Français (1635) and. Académie des sciences (1666).

Humor

Two young ladies met. The more athletic one:
- "What's new?"
- "You wouldn't believe it - I found a very exiting mask!…"

Their husbands:
- Have you heard about peace, freedom and prosperity?
- But of course, everybody is talking about this.

The Amphitheatrum Flavium (Colosseum, 80 AD, left), the **Arch of Constantine (315 AD, right)** and a carabiniere wedding photo event.

Our Future is Sustainable Peace, Freedom and Prosperity

People want:

NOT to destroy anything – they want to build houses, schools, hospitals, and many other strict necessary things, for a better life.

NOT AI, machine learning or 5G for war – all must be for peace only.

NOT hypersonic missiles for war – people want hypersonic airplanes for passengers and cargo.

NOT seabed and NOT space for war – people's seabed and space are for peace only.

NOT beaming solar power from space to Earth for war – people want solar power only for heating their houses, and for other peaceful purposes

NOT space for war – space is people's property to be used for peace only

NOT 5G for war – 5G is only for people's benefit

NOT AI for war

NOT virtual reality for war

NOT lasers for war

NOT precision sensors for war

NOT combat aircraft for war

NOT ballistic nuclear missiles for war

NOT warfare

NOT machine learning for war

NOT battlefield

NOT satellites for war

NOT invasion beaches

NOT hypersonic missile, only hypersonic civilian airplanes, for people's use.

NOT expeditionary forces, only expeditionary friendly people to help other people

NOT special operations, only special medical assistance for people

NOT transforming data into a warfighting tool for death – people want all warfighting death-oriented junk transformed in peace-embracing joyful and useful tools for better life.

All people want to be healthy, not under the stress and anxiety of having a war.

Huge resources are allocated for war, instead of working for people.

Advanced technologies are used for war, instead of improving people's lives.

Space is used for war, instead of activities to help people.

USA, the west side, with the main entrance, of Mount Washington Resort, Bretton Woods, New Hampshire, USA, where the United Nations Monetary and Financial Conference took place in July 1944.

Bibliography

"The Histories" by Polybius

"Discours de la Méthode" by René Descartes

"Meditationes de prima philosophia" by René Descartes

"Philosophiae Naturalis Principia Mathematica" by Isaac Newton

Chinese encyclopedia Gujin Tushu Jicheng (Imperial Encyclopedia)

"Encyclopédie" by Jean-Baptiste le Rond d'Alembert and Denis Diderot

"Encyclopaedia Britannica" by over 4,400 contributors

"Encyclopedia Americana" by Francis Lieber

Other sources include: UPI, CNBC, AP, Nasdaq, Reuters, EDGAR, AFP, Recode, Europa Press, Bloomberg News, Fox News, USA, Deutsche Presse-Agentur, MSNBC, BBC, Australian Associated Press, Agência Brasil, The Canadian Press (La Presse Canadienne), Middle East News Agency, Baltic News Service, Suomen Tietotoimisto, Athens-Macedonian News Agency, Asian News International, Inter Press Service, Kyodo News, Notimex, Algemeen Nederlands Persbureau, AGERPRES, Newsis, Tidningarnas Telegrambyrå, Swiss Telegraphic Agency, Central News Agency, ANKA news agency, Agenzia Fides

Michael M. Dediu is also the author of these books (which can be found on Amazon.com, and www.derc.com):

1. Aphorisms and quotations – with examples and explanations
2. Axioms, aphorisms and quotations – with examples and explanations
3. 100 Great Personalities and their Quotations
4. Professor Petre P. Teodorescu – A Great Mathematician and Engineer
5. Professor Ioan Goia – A Dedicated Engineering Professor
6. Venice (Venezia) – a new perspective. A short presentation with photographs
7. La Serenissima (Venice) - a new photographic perspective. A short presentation with many photos

8. Grand Canal – Venice. A new photographic viewpoint. A short presentation with many photos

9. Piazza San Marco – Venice. A different photographic view. A short presentation with many photos

10. Roma (Rome) - La Città Eterna. A new photographic view. A short presentation with many photos

11. Why is Rome so Fascinating? A short presentation with many photos

12. Rome, Boston and Helsinki. A short photographic presentation

13. Rome and Tokyo – two captivating cities. A short photographic presentation

14. Beautiful Places on Earth – A new photographic presentation

15. From Niagara Falls to Mount Fuji via Rome - A novel photographic presentation

16. From the USA and Canada to Italy and Japan - A fresh photographic presentation

17. Paris – Why So Many Call This City Mon Amour - A lovely photographic presentation

18. The City of Light – Paris (La Ville-Lumière) - A kaleidoscopic photographic presentation

19. Paris (Lutetia Parisiorum) – the romance capital of the world - A kaleidoscopic photographic view

20. Paris and Tokyo – a joyful photographic presentation. With a preamble about the Universe

21. From USA to Japan via Canada – A cheerful photographic documentary

22. 200 Wonderful Places, In The Last 50 Years – A personal photographic documentary

23. Must see places in USA and Japan - A kaleidoscopic photographic documentary

24. Grandeurs of the World - A kaleidoscopic photographic documentary

25. Corneliu Leu – writer on the same wavelength as Mark Twain. An American viewpoint

26. From Berkeley to Pompeii via Rome – A kaleidoscopic photographic documentary

27. From America to Europe via Japan - A kaleidoscopic photographic documentary

28. Discover America and Japan - A photographic documentary

29. J. R. Lucas – philosopher on a creative parallel with Plato, An American viewpoint

30. From America to Switzerland via France - A photographic documentary

31. From Bretton Woods to New York via Cape Cod - A photographic documentary

32. Splendid Places on the Atlantic Coast of the U. S. A. - A photographic documentary

33. Fourteen nice Cities on three Continents - A photographic documentary

34. 17 Picturesque Cities on the World Map - A photographic documentary

35. Unforgettable Places from Four Continents, including Trump buildings - A photographic documentary

36. Dediu Newsletter, Volume 1, Number 1, 6 December 2016 – Monthly news, review, comments and suggestions for a better and wiser world

37. Dediu Newsletter, Volume 1, Number 2, 6 January 2017 (available also at www.derc.com).

38. Dediu Newsletter, Volume 1, Number 3, 6 February 2017 (available at www.derc.com).

39. London and Greenwich, - A photographic documentary

40. Dediu Newsletter, Volume 1, Number 4, 6 March 2017 (available also at www.derc.com).

41. Dediu Newsletter, Volume 1, Number 5, 6 April 2017 (available also at www.derc.com).

42. Dediu Newsletter, Volume 1, Number 6, 6 May 2017 (available also at www.derc.com).

43. Dediu Newsletter, Volume 1, Number 7, 6 June 2017 (available also at www.derc.com).

44. London, Oxford and Cambridge, A photographic documentary

45. Dediu Newsletter, Volume 1, Number 8, 6 July 2017 (available also at www.derc.com).

46. Dediu Newsletter, Volume 1, Number 9, 6 August 2017 (available also at www.derc.com).

47. Dediu Newsletter, Volume 1, Number 10, 6 September 2017 (available also at www.derc.com).

48. Three Great Professors: President Woodrow Wilson, Historian German Arciniegas, and Mathematician Gheorghe Vranceanu – A chronological and photographic documentary

49. Dediu Newsletter, Volume 1, Number 11, 6 October 2017 (available also at www.derc.com).

50. Dediu Newsletter, Volume 1, Number 12, 6 November 2017 (available also at www.derc.com).

51. Dediu Newsletter, Volume 2, Number 1 (13), 6 December 2017 (available also at www.derc.com).

52. Two Great Leaders: Augustus and George Washington - A chronological and photographic documentary

53. Dediu Newsletter, Volume 2, Number 2 (14), 6 January 2018 (available also at www.derc.com).

54. Newton, Benjamin Franklin, and Gauss, A chronological and photographic documentary

55. Dediu Newsletter, Volume 2, Number 3 (15), 6 February 2018 (available also at www.derc.com).

56. 2017: World Top Events, But Many Little Known, A chronological and photographic documentary

57. Dediu Newsletter, Volume 2, Number 4 (16), 6 March 2018 (available also at www.derc.com).

58. Vergilius, Horatius, Ovidius, and Shakespeare - A chronological and photographic documentary.

59. Dediu Newsletter, Volume 2, Number 5 (17), 6 April 2018 (available also at www.derc.com).

60. Dediu Newsletter, Volume 2, Number 6 (18), 6 May 2018 (available also at www.derc.com).

61. Vivaldi, Bach, Mozart, and Verdi - A chronological and photographic documentary.

62. Dediu Newsletter, Volume 2, Number 7 (19), 6 June 2018 (available also at www.derc.com).

63. Dediu Newsletter, Volume 2, Number 8 (20), 6 July 2018 (available also at www.derc.com).

64. Dediu Newsletter, Volume 2, Number 9 (21), 6 August 2018 (available also at www.derc.com).

65. World History, a new perspective - A chronological and photographic documentary.

66. World Humor History with over 100 Jokes, a new perspective - A chronological and photographic documentary

67. Dediu Newsletter, Volume 2, Number 10 (22), 6 September 2018 (available also at www.derc.com).

68. Dediu Newsletter, Volume 2, Number 11 (23), 6 October 2018 (available also at www.derc.com).

69. Dediu Newsletter, Volume 2, Number 12 (24), 6 November 2018

70. Da Vinci, Michelangelo, Rembrandt, Rodin - A chronological and photographic documentary

71. Dediu Newsletter, Volume 3, Number 1 (25), 6 December 2018

72. Dediu Newsletter, Volume 3, Number 2 (26), 6 January 2019

73. From Euclid to Edison – revelries in the past 75 years - A chronological and photographic documentary

74. – Socrates to Churchill Aphorisms celebrated after 1960 - A chronological and photographic documentary

75. - Dediu Newsletter, Volume 3, Number 3 (27), 6 February 2019

76. – Hippocrates to Fleming: Medicine History celebrated after 1943 - A chronological and photographic documentary

77. - Dediu Newsletter, Volume 3, Number 4 (28), 6 March 2019

78. - Dediu Newsletter, Volume 3, Number 5 (29), 6 April 2019

79 – Archimedes to Ford: Invention History celebrated after 1943 - A chronological and photographic documentary

80 - Dediu Newsletter, Volume 3, Number 6 (30), 6 May 2019

81 – Sutherland to Pavarotti: Great Singers History - A chronological and photographic documentary

82 - Dediu Newsletter, Volume 3, Number 7 (31), 6 June 2019

83 - Dediu Newsletter, Volume 3, Number 8 (32), 6 July 2019

84 – Augustus to Rockefeller: History of the Wealthiest People - A chronological and photographic documentary

85 - Dediu Newsletter, Volume 3, Number 9 (33), 6 August 2019

86 – Pythagoras to Fermi: History of Science - A chronological and photographic documentary

87 - Dediu Newsletter, Volume 3, Number 10 (34), 6 September 2019

88 – Our Future is Sustainable Peace and Prosperity – Moving from conflicts to harmony and peace

89 - Dediu Newsletter, Volume 3, Number 11 (35), 6 October 2019 – World Monthly Report with news

90 – Our Future Depends on Good World Educations – Moving from frail education to solid education

91 - Dediu Newsletter, Volume 3, Number 12 (36), 6 November 2019 – World Monthly Report with News and Suggestions for Sustainable Peace, Freedom and Prosperity

92 – Friendly, Helpful & Smart World Management - Moving from bureaucracy to responsive world management

93 – If You Want Peace, Prepare for Peace! – Moving from preparation for war to preparation for peace

94 - Dediu Newsletter, Volume 4, Number 1 (37), 6 December 2019 – World Monthly Report with News and Suggestions for Sustainable Peace, Freedom and Prosperity

95 – World with One Country & its Ten Friendly Regions - Moving from 195 disagreeing countries, to 1 country with 10 collaborating regions

96 - Dediu Newsletter, Volume 4, Number 2 (38), 6 January 2020 – World Monthly Report with News and Suggestions for Sustainable Peace, Freedom and Prosperity

97 – After 10,000 Years of Conflicts, People want 10,000 Years of Harmony - Moving from continuous wars to stable peace

98 - Dediu Newsletter, Volume 4, Number 3 (39), 6 February 2020 – World Monthly Report with News and Suggestions for Sustainable Peace, Freedom and Prosperity

99 – The Constitution of the World – Moving from many unsustainable constitutions, to just one Constitution of the World

100 - Dediu Newsletter, Volume 4, Number 4 (40), 6 March 2020 – World Monthly Report with News and Suggestions for Sustainable Peace, Freedom and Prosperity

101 - Dediu Newsletter, Volume 4, Number 5 (41), 6 April 2020 – World Monthly Report

102 - Dediu Newsletter, Volume 4, Number 6 (42), 6 May 2020 – World Monthly Report

103 – World Constitution Implementation – Moving from violent changes, to smooth transition to the Constitution of the World

104 - Dediu Newsletter, Volume 4, Number 7 (43), 6 June 2020 – World Monthly Report

105 - Dediu Newsletter, Volume 4, Number 8 (44), 6 July 2020 – World Monthly Report

106 - It is getting truer and truer – we urgently need the World Constitution: Moving from anarchic changes, to balanced transition to the Constitution of the World

107 - Dediu Newsletter, Volume 4, Number 9 (45), 6 August 2020 – World Monthly Report

108 - World Constitution with Lovely Comments - Moving from many suboptimal constitutions to the much better Constitution of the World

109 - Dediu Newsletter, Volume 4, Number 10 (46), 6 September 2020 – World Monthly Report

110 – World Constitution with Questions & Answers – Moving from many obsolete constitutions to the much better Constitution of the World

111 - Dediu Newsletter, Volume 4, Number 11 (47), 6 October 2020 – World Monthly Report

112 - World Projects - Moving from minor projects to great projects for the World

Mathematical Reviews: American Mathematical Society (AMS) sent for review, over the years, 298 mathematical research papers and books, to Michael M. Dediu, and his reviews where published in the Mathematical Reviews of the AMS.

Italy, Roma (753 BC, one of the oldest occupied cities in Europe, called Roma Aeterna (The Eternal City) and Caput Mundi (Capital of the World)), southeast of Piazza del Popolo (1822, by Giuseppe Valadier, inside the northern gate in the Aurelian Walls, the Porta Flaminia, now called the Porta del Popolo), near Via del Babuino (opened in 1525 as the Via Paolina) and the church Santa Maria in Montesanto (1679, begun by Rainaldi and completed by Bernini and Fontana), the statue of the Goddess of Abundance.

www.ingramcontent.com/pod-product-compliance
Lightning Source LLC
Chambersburg PA
CBHW041713200326
41519CB00001B/150